# HENRI
# MATISSE

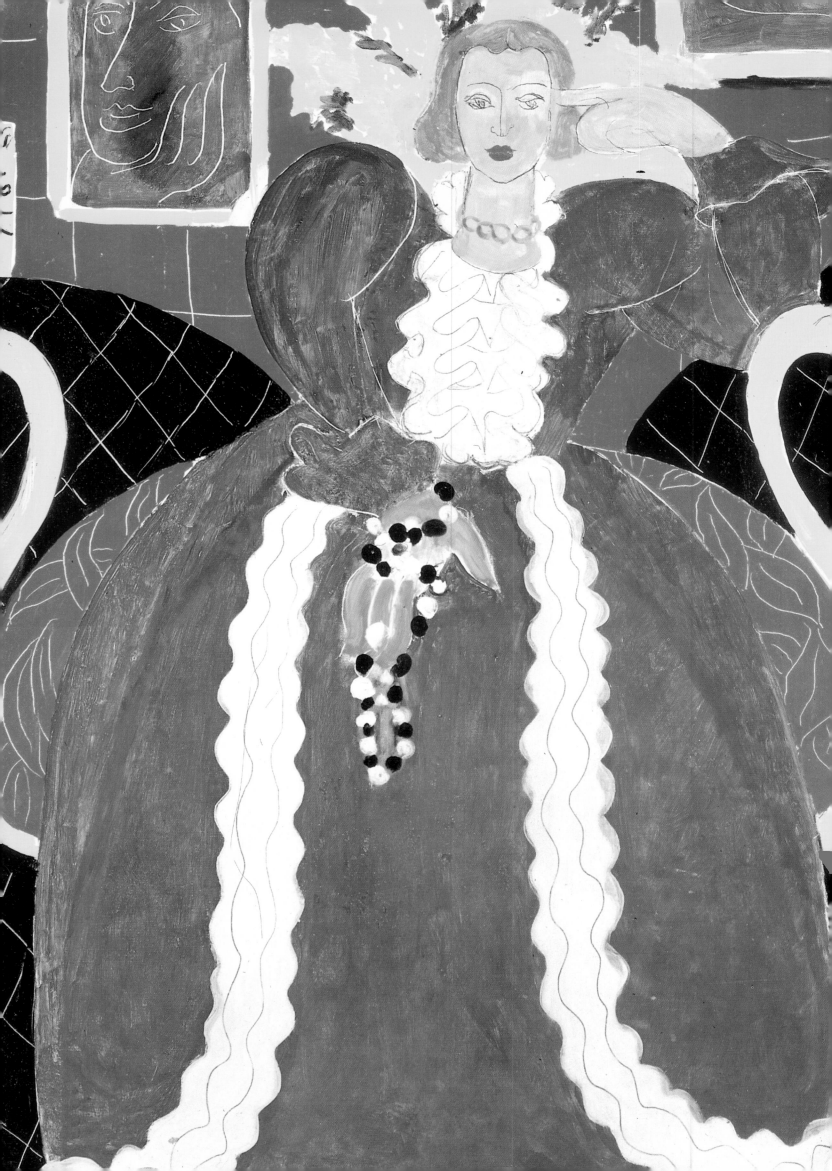

# HENRI MATISSE

## FRANK MILNER

BARNES
&NOBLE
BOOKS
NEW YORK

This edition published by
Barnes and Noble Inc.,
by arrangement with Brompton
Books Corporation.

Produced by Brompton Books
Corporation
15 Sherwood Place
Greenwich, CT 06830

ISBN 1-56619-465-2

Printed in Spain

FOR A DEAR AUNT—NORAH

PAGE 1 **Self-Portrait,** 1918
Collection Musée Matisse,
Le Cateau-Cambrésis

PAGE 2 **Lady in Blue** (detail), 1937,
Philadelphia Museum of Art,
Gift of Mrs John Wintersteen

BELOW **Polynesia, La Mer,** 1946
Musée National d'Art Moderne,
Centre Georges Pompidou, Paris

# CONTENTS

Introduction                                          6

Woman Reading                                        18
Breton Village (The Pigkeeper)                       19
Interior with a Top Hat                              20
The Dinner Table                                     22
Still Life (after Chardin's 'Ray')                   24
The Bridge                                           25
First Orange Still Life                              26
Street in Arcueil                                    28
Male Nude in the Studio                              30
Self-Portrait                                        31
Notre Dame                                           32
Carmelina                                            33
Still Life with Oranges                              34
The Luxembourg Gardens                               36
Place des Lices, St Tropex                           38
Open Window, Collioure                               40
Femme au Chapeau                                     41
Notre Dame                                           42
Luxe, Calme et Volupté                               44
Portrait with the Green Stripe: Madame
    Matisse                                          45
Landscape at Collioure                               46
Self-Portrait                                        48
Oil Sketch for 'The Joy of Life'                     49
Blue Nude: Souvenir of Biskra                        50
La Berge                                             52
Still Life with Geranium Plant and Fruit             53
Greta Moll                                           54
Luxe 1                                               55
The Dinner Table: Harmony in Red                     56
Music                                                58
Dance                                                60
Fruit, Flowers and 'Dance'                           62
Still Life with Bronze and Fruit                     64
The Pink Studio                                       66
The Conversation                                     68
Interior with Aubergines                             70
The Goldfish                                         71
The Painter's Family                                 72
On the Terrace                                       74
Window at Tangier                                    75

The Casbah Gate                                      76
Gray Nude with Bracelet                              77
Arab Café                                            78
Portrait of Madame Matisse                           79
Open Window, Collioure                               80
Mademoiselle Yvonne Landsberg                        81
Composition: The Yellow Curtain                      82
Bathers by a River                                   84
The Window                                           86
Greta Prozor                                         87
Tree near Trivaux Pond                               88
Head of Laurette and a Cup of Coffee                 89
The Painter and his Model                            90
My Room at the Beau Rivage                           91
Self-Portrait                                        92
Plaster Torso and Bouquet of Flowers                 93
The Artist and his Model                             94
Tea                                                  96
Woman before an Aquarium                             98
Still Life: Dahlias and a White Book                100
Odalisque, Half-length: The Tattoo                  101
The Anemones                                         102
Decorative Figure on an Ornamental
    Background                                      104
The Yellow Dress                                    105
Odalisque                                           106
Nature Morte au Buffet Vert                         108
Large Reclining Nude                                110
Dance 1                                             112
Nu au Fauteuil, Plante Verte                        114
Lady in Blue                                        115
Music                                               116
Interior with Etruscan Vase                         118
Interior, Yellow and Blue                           120
Polynesia, la Mer                                   121
The Sorrow of the King                              122
Interior with Egyptian Curtain                      124
Zulma                                               125
Blue Nude 3                                         126
The Snail                                           127

Acknowledgments                                     128
Select Bibliography                                 128

# INTRODUCTION

'My art is not of the intellect.' 'What I dream of is an art of balance and purity, of serenity devoid of troubling and depressing subject matter, an art which could be for every mental worker – for the businessman, as well as the man of letters, for example, a soothing calming influence upon the mind, something like a good armchair which provides relaxation for physical fatigue.' The views of Henri Matisse (1869-1954), supreme colorist of the twentieth century, recorded in over 40 written statements, radio interviews and newspaper articles, remained notably consistent. From his 1908 *Notes of a Painter*, the manifesto in which he first made the now notorious comparison of art with an armchair, to his final writings just before his death, Matisse pressed the same arguments. 'I haven't changed – different means – but I'm looking for the same things.'

Within the traditions of rectangular easel painting Matisse, more perfectly than any other artist, made color work independently of form – intelligently but not, as he said, intellectually. The distinction is important; Matisse wanted a direct emotional impact from his color. 'Drawing is the precision of thought,' he wrote, 'drawing belongs to the world of the Spirit, color to the world of the Senses.'

Matisse achieved his goals partly by staying very close to established, even conventional, modes of pictorial structure and balance. Innovation and tradition are always yoked in his art. *Dance* of 1910, for example, a group of connected dancing figures, has pictorial affinities with early Renaissance processional frescoes, while the magnificent *Pink Studio* of 1911 is as carefully balanced as a Poussin. *Tea* of 1919 is conceived and composed like any number of eighteenth-century conversation pieces; *Lady in Blue* (1937) is comparable with Ingres' *Madame Moitessier*, whose very pose and hand gestures it seems to imitate. What is different in all these, of course, is the saturated pure color, simplifications of form, and deployment of fields of color as a substitute for recessive space and depth. Nevertheless the connections remain. 'I owe my art to all past painters,' stated Matisse: 'I copied Old Masters in the Louvre when I was young, grasping their thinking by studying their technique. In the realm of modern art it is to Cézanne that I owe the greatest debt.'

Matisse's training as an artist, following a legal career abandoned after four years, was principally under the supervision of the symbolist painter Gustave Moreau (1826-98). Moreau's complex biblical and mythological pictures did not interest Matisse, but Moreau was also a superb and stimulating teacher: 'A cultivated man who encouraged his pupils to study every kind of painting,' was how Matisse later described him. As early as 1858, while a student in Rome, Moreau had debated with Degas about how color alone might play the central role in a picture, and he raised this question again with the second genius to come under his influence.

The avant-garde artistic climate in Paris during the 1890s was full of discussion about new ways of liberating and intensifying color in pictures. It is easier, however, to list the various branches of modernity that Matisse rejected in this period than those to which he subscribed. He was not, for example, interested in metropolitan naturalism like his contemporaries Lautrec and Forain, nor in the fin-de-siècle delights of Symbolism, nor in Expressive color as used by Gauguin and his followers. Until the mid 1890s Matisse was developing into a painter of rather stolid, intimate, interior views.

From 1896 Matisse became interested in the sculpture of Rodin (whose pupil he unsuccessfully attempted to become) and in the paintings of Cézanne, and bought works by both. His own landscapes became loosely-textured, more impressionistic, and from 1898 he began to introduce apparently arbitrary coloring – emeralds, purples, oranges and cobalts. Several of his

FAR LEFT The painter as patriarch.

ABOVE LEFT Matisse owned a version of this bust of Henri Rochefort by Rodin, which originally belonged to Manet.

ABOVE RIGHT Matisse's bronze *Le Serf*, c. 1900, was strongly influenced by Rodin's modeling.

nudes around 1900 have faceted, Cézannesque surfaces and use dissonant colors and striking Rodinesque stances. His sculptures also evoke Rodin's modeling. Matisse's landscapes from the period 1900-03 suggest, however, that it was the touch of Cézanne that primarily dictated his own approach.

The big change in Matisse's art came in 1904. Having read Paul Signac's essay 'De Delacroix au Neo-Impressionisme' in 1899, he spent the summer of 1904 at Signac's house in St Tropez, painting in the 'Divisionist' or 'Neo-Impressionist' style. *Luxe, Calme et Volupté*, an arcadian vision of indolence on the Mediterranean shoreline, is painted in the distinctive caterpillar-like lines and calculated color contrasts and complementaries favored by Signac and his followers. It is the most important work Matisse painted during what turned out to be a brief flirtation with Neo-Impressionism. In the following year, under the influence of the young artist André Derain (1880-1954), Matisse painted a series of altogether more audaciously vibrant pictures. These included views of Collioure and portraits of himself and Madame Matisse. They are roughly textured and without tonal contrast, and their strident green and red dissonances helped earn for Matisse and some of his fellow artists the nickname 'Fauve' (wild beast) when they were exhibited at the Salon des Indépendants in 1906.

Fauvism held Matisse for about two years, then he distanced himself from its jarring reverberations and emotional intensity. 'The mannerisms of a style can turn against itself,' he later reflected, and from 1907 his painting became more simplified. Drawing – 'essential lines' – became clearer, colors, fewer and more precisely related. 'Just three colors on a large panel of dancers, blue for the sky, pink for the bodies, green for the hill,' was how he summed up the monumental pair of *Dance* and *Music* made for the Russian collector Schukin.

Matisse often described his pictures as 'condensed sensations'. Almost all his work depicts nature, or is figurative, but he made it clear that nature did not dictate its own appearance in his pictures. There is, for example, little true weather in a Matisse landscape, little psychological penetration in his portraits or nudes. Subordinating the motif *was* very important for him. 'Cézanne was a moment in art,' he wrote, 'Sisley a movement in nature.' It has been suggested that, when Matisse made light into solid colored form and made intense color evoke space, he was inspired by strong Mediterranean sunshine or the noonday glare on a North African souk. However he did not share any of the naturalistic transcriptive intentions of artists like Monet, Delacroix or even Renoir, all of whom had been seduced into painting the southern landscape and its light. 'A

ABOVE Cézanne's *Three Bathers*, c. 1880, bought by the impecunious young Matisse, had a major effect upon his own arcadian nude pictures.

RIGHT *The Joy of Life*, 1905-06, Matisse's most important mature fauve painting.

work of art,' he argued, 'must carry within itself its complete significance and impose that on the spectator even before the subject is apparent.' He went so far as to suggest that during the period 1907 to 1912 he was not even painting subjects.

Several of the great pictures of this period, including *The Dinner Table: Harmony in Red* (1908) and *Pink Studio* (1911), explored the decorative use of color on a grand scale. Matisse studied pattern from several cultures: in 1910 he looked at Spanish and Moorish tiles and fabrics; in 1911 he scrutinized Persian miniatures and Russian icons. Islamic art in particular, he said, had helped to reveal the full possibilities of his own sensations. Those of his pictures from this period in which pulsating red predominates strongly evoke Oriental carpets. Instead of a rug's simple left-to-right and top-to-bottom balance, however, a complex harmony of volumes and lines sits on the field of color, and the usual little decorative peacocks and flowers are replaced by his studio and dining-room bric-à-brac.

Matisse worked in different styles at this period. While the principal thrust of his energies was toward the realization of a purely decorative art – Moreau's legacy, so to speak – it was also impossible for him to ignore the new concerns with space that Picasso and Braque were raising in their Cubist explorations – part of Cézanne's legacy. For Matisse the art of Cézanne, with its overlapping syncopated brushstrokes, principally evoked light. For Picasso, on the other hand, Cézanne's distinctive touch represented shifting foci which inspired his own interest in multiple viewpoints and more complex descriptions of volume. A characteristic of Cubist art was to empty color out of pictures in order to

concentrate on volume. From 1911, in certain pictures, Matisse used some parts of the Cubist vocabulary: solid black cast shadows, sickle-shaped and triangular modeling shadows, and darker tonalities. Even in bright Moroccan views, like *The Casbah Gate* of 1912, there is a new concern with orthogonals and solid shadow. This experimentation reached a climax in 1914-16; *Composition: The Yellow Curtain* is reduced to a few lines, simplified rectangular solids and drab colors, while *Mademoiselle Yvonne Landsberg* of 1914, with its nimbus of dynamic arcing lines, might almost be a Futurist picture. Matisse never, however, tried to paint multiple viewpoints.

Some of Matisse's greatest art was produced working against the grain of Cubism. Expressionism he could dismiss, but Cubism represented an assault upon the primacy of color, and so upon his own artistic position. He dealt with it by trying to absorb it. Despite the 1908 disclaimer that he wished for a soothing art, Cubist-connected pictures such as *The Conversation* (1911), *Portrait of Madame Matisse* (1913), *Open Window, Collioure* (1914) are far from calming. Their potency derives not from any radiant effusion of light as color, but from their taut schematic interconnections of volume and mass. They are cerebral pictures; Matisse playing

Cubism's game to win. It has been suggested that the darker tones of certain pictures at this time are connected with Matisse's distress about the First World War and its devastating effects upon France. While worth considering, even accepting, this hypothesis, it scarcely explains the radical nature of his spatial experimentation up to 1916.

In 1917 Matisse moved south to Nice and lived in a series of hotel rooms and lodgings before settling into a permanent apartment. Aged 50 and selling well, he spent most of the next decade on the Riviera coast, away from the complexity of contending innovations in Paris. His motifs remained the familiar ensembles of naked model, open window, large-patterned fabrics, vases of flowers and fruit still lifes, but his pictures became smaller, and with a more traditional spatial structure. Flesh is softly modeled and any dissonant faceting avoided. Despite glimpses of the intense Mediterranean blue sun and sky, seen through half-shuttered windows, and the occasional, almost palpably solid, shafts of bright southern light, redolent of that in the great Moroccan pictures of 1911

LEFT Picasso's *Three Women*,
1907-08. Cubist spatial
experimentation like this led
Matisse to modify his art c.
1911-15.

RIGHT Matisse drawing the nude
Villa Alesia, Paris, summer 1939

and 1912, these works as a group are Matisse's most hermetic: the artist in retreat, a closed self-immersion in the studied observation of his beloved model, in interior view after interior view. It has been usual among critics to view the 1920s as a falling-off in Matisse's creativity, to suggest that these pictures, which sold in increasing numbers to American collectors, were formulaic, to type, and conveniently sized for integration into almost any domestic environment. Pictures that cost 5000 francs in 1917 were selling for ten times that by 1928. In most monographs on Matisse this decade figures least. Politer

commentators suggest that he was taking stock, that he was going through a conservative and stylized classical phase akin to Picasso's contemporaneous absorption with antique and classical themes.

Matisse took a new model, Henriette Darricarrére, at the start of the 1920s. From 1921 to 1927 she became his *odalisque*, acting out his intimate, exotic and vaguely Oriental fantasies. *Decorative Figure on an Ornamental Background* is the consummate achievement in this vein, and the most complete fusion of a single figure and a highly decorative background in Matisse's entire oeuvre.

Stripped to linear essentials, this figure is also the prototype for the great *papier collé* blue nudes of the early 1950s. Matisse's defenders have tended to suggest that his odalisques are serene and desexualized arrangements of form. More recently, feminist cultural historians have highlighted their peculiarly obsessive scrutiny of female passivity.

In the later 1920s Matisse painted less. The fillip that lifted him and re-engaged his interest in painting was a new commission, the biggest of his life. Dr Arthur C Barnes, a Philadelphia physician turned businessman in antiseptics, was a voracious collector of avant-garde European art. For his newly-built foundation at Merion, Pennsylvania, Matisse painted three huge semi-circular connected canvases, *Dance* (1931-33). Two versions exist; the first was a few inches too short, so Matisse radically altered his second design, adding two figures. In concept they are not dissimilar to the 1909 *Dance* painted for Schukin; six and eight figures united in rhythmic harmony cavort in naked ecstasy. It is in essence a large tinted drawing, a key work marking the genesis of a new linear grammar in Matisse's art. Flatness and linearity, when used earlier, had invariably been accompanied by delicious visual elisions of stroke to stroke, so that the lingering pleasure of surface facture remained for the spectator. Now the emphasis is on

circumscribing, containing, and the incised line. *Large Reclining Nude* (1935) and *Lady in Blue* (1937) are both in this mode. In the latter Matisse incises line into paint like white grout lines around floor tiles. For the Barnes painting he used large pre-painted paper cut-outs to help organize the positioning of color masses. A decade before ill-health forced him to adopt cut paper as his principal creative medium, Matisse was already moving toward the hieratic flatness of stained glass.

From 1930 Matisse turned increasingly to book illustration, doing etchings for editions of Stéphane Mallarmé's *Poems* and James Joyce's *Ulysses*. He also designed sets in 1939 for the Ballet Russe's *Rouge et Noir*, in which he used lunette-like flat arches and flat geometric forms akin to the Barnes mural. As ever with Matisse, one project fed into another. In the late 1930s he wrote some of the fullest statements of his artistic intention since 1908. Affirming the new place of drawing in his work, he wrote:

In spite of the absence of shadow and half-tones expressed by hatching, I do not renounce the play of values and modulations. I modulate with variations in the weight of line and above all with the area it delimits on white paper . . . To sum up I work *without a theory* . . . as Chardin used to say 'I add until it looks right'.

ABOVE Ill and bedbound. Matisse continued working using cut colored paper, c. 1950.

ABOVE *The Dance*, Matisse's largest picture for the Barnes Foundation, Merion, 1931-33

Matisse's final phase, from his severe illness in 1940 until his death in 1954, was heroic and innovative. His inter-war reputation, built up by private collectors, was augmented by increased museum collecting and scholarship. After 1940 Matisse again painted less. Those works that he did produce are looser re-workings of earlier themes. *Interior, Yellow and Blue* (1946) and *Interior with Egyptian Curtain* (1948) evoke the great interiors of 1911, with their simple zigzagged black lines and outline, but with fewer patterns and simpler viewpoints. The control and command is still evident, but these are not great paintings. Matisse's strength in handling line and color was expressed elsewhere at this time with cut-out paper. 'Like sculpting with scissors,'

was how he described the expressive freedom that he gained from working on a large scale with pre-colored paper, cut out then stuck down. The large blue nudes, such as *Zulma* (1950) and similar figures, hark back to the arcadian pictures of 1906-08, and suggest that Matisse had at last broken with the use of the model. He also crossed the divide into abstraction, a development that flowed from the series of abstract evocations of music that he had done as brightly-colored stencil prints for the publication *Jazz*.

Although Matisse may have aspired to create a purely decorative art, even the major, almost abstract works of this period still link with nature. In *The Snail* (1952-53),

for example the spiral of a shell is represented by a vortex of colored rectangles. At the time he wrote:

When I am in direct accord with my sensations of nature I feel that I am entitled to depart from them, the better to register what I feel. For me nature is always present. As in love, it all depends upon what the artist unconsciously projects on all that he sees. The quality of this projection rather than the presence of a living person is what gives an artist's vision its life.

In 1948 Matisse painted a figure of St Dominic in the church of Notre-Dame-de-Toute-Grâce at Assy. Between 1948 and 1951 he worked on the structure and decoration of a chapel for a group of nuns at Vence. Both

LEFT *Seated Nude*, 1925, posed by Henriette Darricarrère, is more classical, less Rodinesque in form.

RIGHT AND BELOW Furnishings and stained glass for the chapel at Vence, 1948-51.

projects were tokens of thanksgiving to the Dominicans for the nursing that he had received when he was ill, rather than acts of personal worship. Matisse was not a Catholic and his own views on religion were eclectic. Not altogether surprisingly, they were linked with the universalist aspirations that he had for his own art. 'The love of creation and the work to be made is my single religion,' he said in 1952 when quizzed about his beliefs. The vestments, altar furniture and two stained glass windows, which are usually considered the best part of

the entire Vence ensemble, were all designed by Matisse. With these windows, which are so close in design to related cut-outs, Matisse achieved in three dimensions what he had already done for half a century in paint: making color work as light.

In 1992, 800,000 visitors attended the New York Museum of Modern Art Matisse exhibition. In 1993, at the Pompidou Center in Paris, people queued for hours to see the Matisse 1904-1917 show. Since 1986 the National Gallery in Washington has held four major exhibitions solely or in significant part devoted to Matisse's work. It is difficult to believe that his work can become more popular. Critical voices have recently been raised, however, both about these adulatory 'blockbuster' shows and about Matisse and his art. Some have questioned how any art, however joyful, could claim for itself such hermetic isolation from a French cultural and social history that included two world wars.

Others, particularly feminist art historians, have sought to explore the various 'dominations' perceived between Matisse and his depicted models. The recent 1993 Paris exhibition produced interesting scholarly analysis of Matisse's exoticism, which explored his Tangiers pictures within the colonial context of France's declaration in 1911 of Morocco as a protectorate. (Matisse's 1913 show of Moroccan pictures at the Galerie Vernheim-Jeune had a live Riff warrior displayed as a 'splendid barbarian'). Matisse's children are now all dead and there is a change evident in the discretion traditionally maintained about Matisse's illegitimate first daughter, his separation from Madame Matisse and his relationships with his models. It is to be expected that the next decade will see several new contextual 're-readings' of his works.

LEFT *Jazz: Le Toboggan.* 1943. Matisse's first cut-out paper designs were for stencil-printed book illustration.

RIGHT *Composition on a Green Background.* c. 1950.

BELOW Matisse aged 82, in his villa at Vence in 1951.

**Woman Reading,** 1894,
*Oil on canvas, 24¼×18⅞ inches (61.5×47.9cm)*
Musée National d'Art Moderne, Centre Georges Pompidou,
Paris

**Breton Village (The Pig Keeper)**, 1896
*Oil on canvas, 23½×28¾ inches (59.5×73cm)*
Musée Matisse, Nice

**Interior with a Top Hat,** 1896
*Oil on canvas, 25⅝×31⅞ inches (80×94.9cm)*
Private Collection, Paris

**The Dinner Table,** 1897
*Oil on canvas, 38⅞×51½ inches*
*(100×131cm)*
Private Collection, London

**Still Life (after Chardin's 'Ray'),** 1898
*Oil on canvas, 45×55½ inches (115×142cm)*
Collection Musée Matisse, Le Cateau-Cambrésis

**The Bridge,** 1898
*Oil on canvas, 14×11 inches (35.5×28cm)*
Board of Trustees of the National Museums and Galleries on
Merseyside, Walker Art Gallery, Liverpool

**First Orange Still Life,** 1899
*Oil on canvas, 22×28¾ inches
(56×73cm)*
Musée National d'Art Moderne, Centre
Georges Pompidou, Paris

**Street in Arcueil,** 1899
*Oil on canvas, 8⅝×10⅝ inches (22×27cm)*
Statens Museum for Kunst, Copenhagen

**Male Nude in the Studio,** 1899
*Oil on canvas, 14×11 inches (35.5×28cm)*
Collection Musée Matisse, Le Cateau-Cambrésis

**Self-Portrait,** 1900
*Oil on canvas, 21¹/₂×18¹/₈ inches (55×46cm)*
Musée National d'Art Moderne, Centre Georges Pompidou, Paris

ABOVE
**Notre Dame,** 1900
*Oil on canvas, 18¹/₈×14⁷/₈ inches (46×37.7cm)*
Tate Gallery, London

RIGHT
**Carmelina,** 1903
*Oil on canvas, 32×23¹/₄ inches (81.3×59cm)*
Museum of Fine Arts, Boston, Tompkins Collection

32

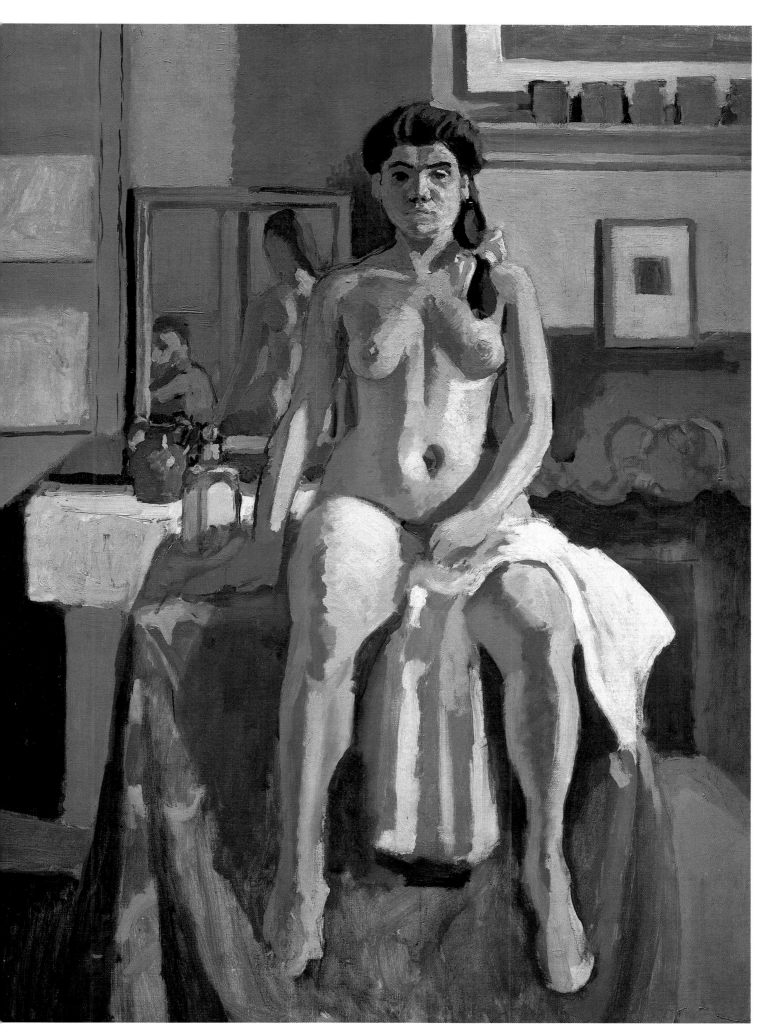

**Still Life with Oranges,** c.1902
*Oil on canvas, 18³/₈×21³/₄ inches (45.7×55.2cm)*
Washington University Gallery of Art, St Louis,
Gift of Mr and Mrs Sydney M Shoenberg Jr, 1962

**The Luxembourg Gardens,**
1901-02
*Oil on canvas, 23½×32¼*
*inches (59.5×81.5cm)*
Hermitage Museum,
St Petersburg

**Place des Lices, St Tropez,** 1904
*Oil on canvas, 20¹/₄×21⁵/₈ inches (46×55cm)*
Statens Museum for Kunst, Copenhagen

ABOVE

**Open Window, Collioure,** 1905

*Oil on canvas, 21³⁄₄×15³⁄₄ inches (55.2×46cm)*

Collection of Mrs John Hay Whitney, New York

RIGHT

**Femme au Chapeau,** 1905

*Oil on canvas, 31³⁄₄×23¹⁄₂ inches (80.6×59.7)*

San Francisco Museum of Modern Art, Bequest of Elise S Haas

**Notre Dame,** 1905
*Oil on canvas, 17½×21½ inches (45×55cm)*
Moderna Museet, Stockholm

**Luxe, Calme, et Volupté,** 1904-05
*Oil on canvas, 37×46 inches (94×117cm)*
Musée National d'Art Moderne, Centre Georges Pompidou, Paris

**Portrait with the Green Stripe: Madame
Matisse,** 1905
*Oil on canvas, 15¾×12¾ inches (40.5×32.5cm)*
Statens Museum for Kunst, Copenhagen

**Landscape at Collioure,** 1905-06,
*Oil on canvas, 23⅜×28¾ inches (59.4×73cm)*
Hermitage Museum, St Petersburg

**Self-Portrait**, 1905-06
*Oil on canvas, 21¼×20¼ inches (55×46cm)*
Statens Museum for Kunst, Copenhagen

**Oil Sketch for 'The Joy of Life',** 1905-06,
*Oil on canvas, 15³/₄×21¹/₄ inches (40.6×54.6cm)*
San Francisco Museum of Modern Art

**Blue Nude (Souvenir de Biskra),** 1907
*Oil on canvas, 36¼×55⅛ inches (92.1×141.1cm)*
Baltimore Museum of Art, The Cone Collection, formed by
Dr Claribel Cone and Miss Etta Cone of Baltimore, Maryland

**La Berge,** 1907
*Oil on canvas, 28½×24 inches (73×60.5cm)*
Offentliche Kunstsammlung Basel, Kunstmuseum

**Still Life with Geranium Plant and Fruit,** 1907
*Oil on canvas, 38½×31½ inches (101.3×82.6cm)*
The Art Institute of Chicago, Joseph Winterbotham Collection 1932-1942

**ABOVE**
**Greta Moll,** 1908
*Oil on canvas, 36½×28¾ inches (93×73.5cm)*
The National Gallery, London

**Luxe I,** 1907
*Oil on canvas, 82¾×54¾ inches (214×143cm)*
Musée National d'Art Moderne,
Centre Georges Pompidou, Paris

**The Dinner Table – Harmony in Red,** 1908
*Oil on canvas, 69¾×85⅞ inches (177.1×218.1cm)*
Hermitage Museum, St Petersburg

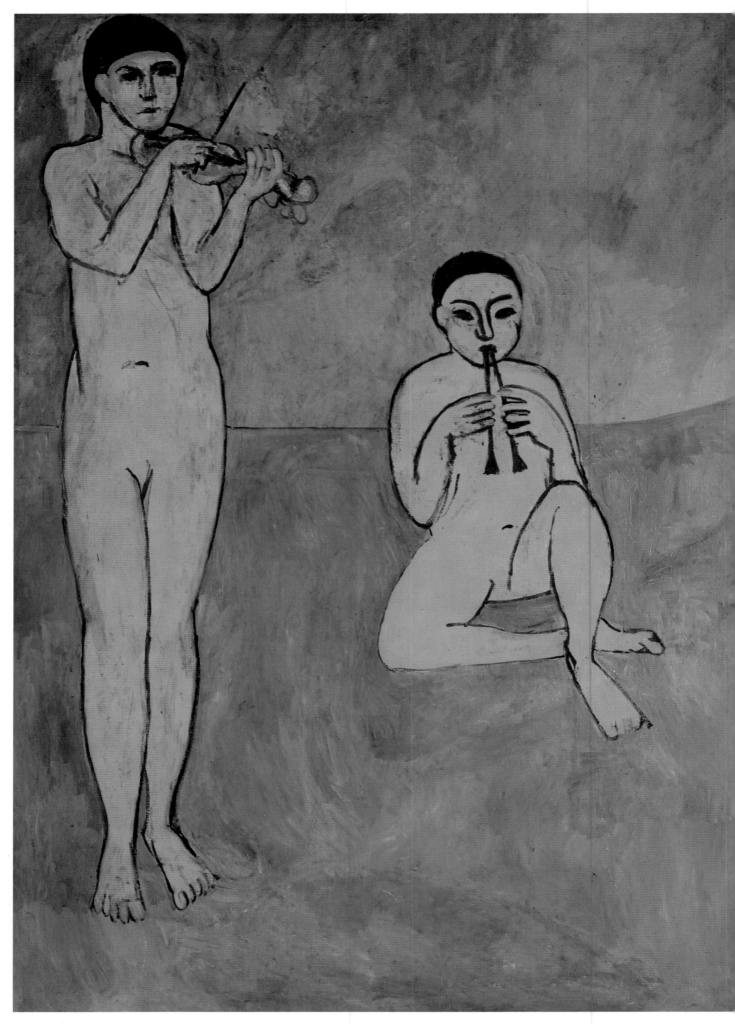

PAGES 58-59:
**Music,** 1910
*Oil on canvas, 101⅝×153½ inches
(260×391cm)*
Hermitage Museum, St Petersburg

PAGES 60-61:
**Dance,** 1910
*Oil on canvas, 101⅝×153½ inches
(260×391cm)*
Hermitage Museum, St Petersburg

RIGHT
**Fruit, Flowers and 'Dance',** 1910
*Oil on canvas, 35½×41¾ inches
(89×116cm)*
Hermitage Museum, St Petersburg

**Still Life with Bronze and Fruit,**
1910
*Oil on canvas, 35³/₈×45¹/₄ inches*
*(90×115cm)*
Pushkin Museum of Fine Art, Moscow

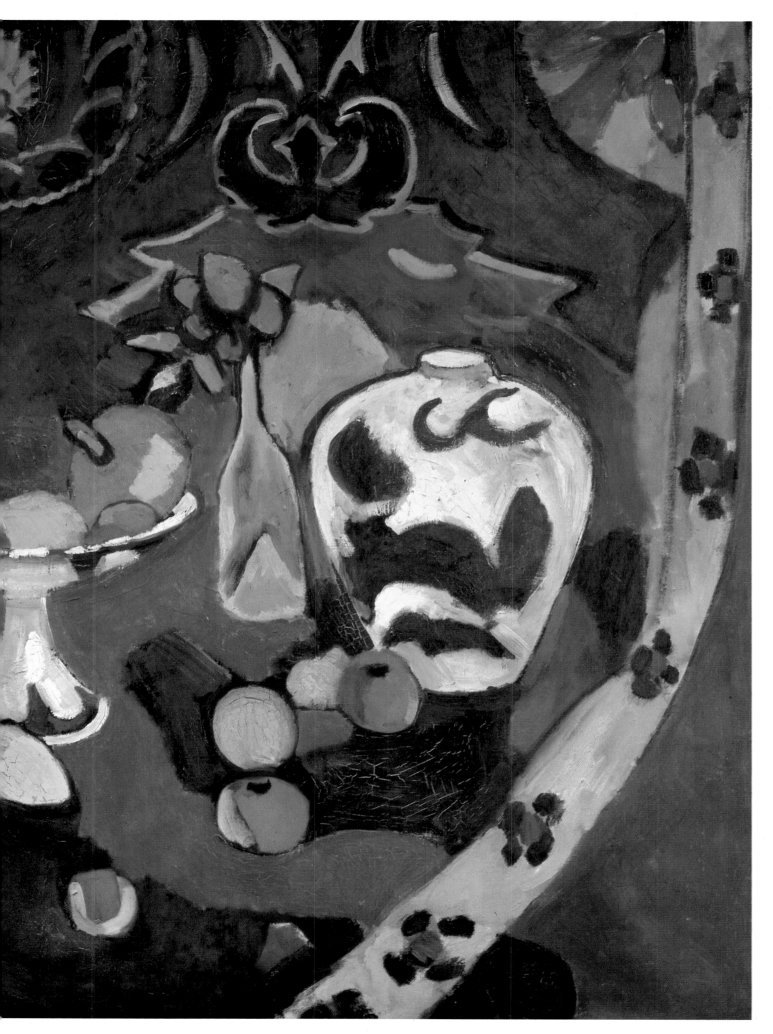

**The Pink Studio,** 1911
*Oil on canvas, 71×86½ inches (179.5×221cm)*
Pushkin Museum of Fine Art, Moscow

**The Conversation,** 1911
*Oil on canvas, 69¾×85½ inches (177×217cm)*
The Hermitage, St Petersburg

**Interior with Aubergines,** 1911
*Distemper on canvas, 83³/₈×96³/₄ inches (212×246cm)*
Musée de Grenoble

**The Goldfish,** 1912
*Oil on canvas, 57⁷/₈×38⁵/₈ inches (147×98cm)*
Pushkin Museum of Fine Art, Moscow

**The Painter's Family,** 1911
*Oil on canvas, 56¼×76⅜ inches
(142×194cm)*
Hermitage Museum, St Petersburg

ABOVE
**On the Terrace,** 1912/13
*Oil on canvas, 45¼×39⅜ inches (115×101cm)*
Pushkin Museum of Fine Arts, Moscow

RIGHT
**Window at Tangier,** 1912-13
*Oil on canvas, 45¼×31⅛ inches (115×80cm)*
Pushkin Museum of Fine Arts, Moscow

LEFT
**The Casbah Gate,** 1912/13
*Oil on canvas, 45⅝×31½ inches (116×80cm)*
Pushkin Museum of Fine Arts, Moscow

ABOVE
**Gray Nude with Bracelet,** 1913
Oil on canvas, 29¼×25 inches (75×61cm)
Private Collection, on loan to Kunsthaus, Zürich

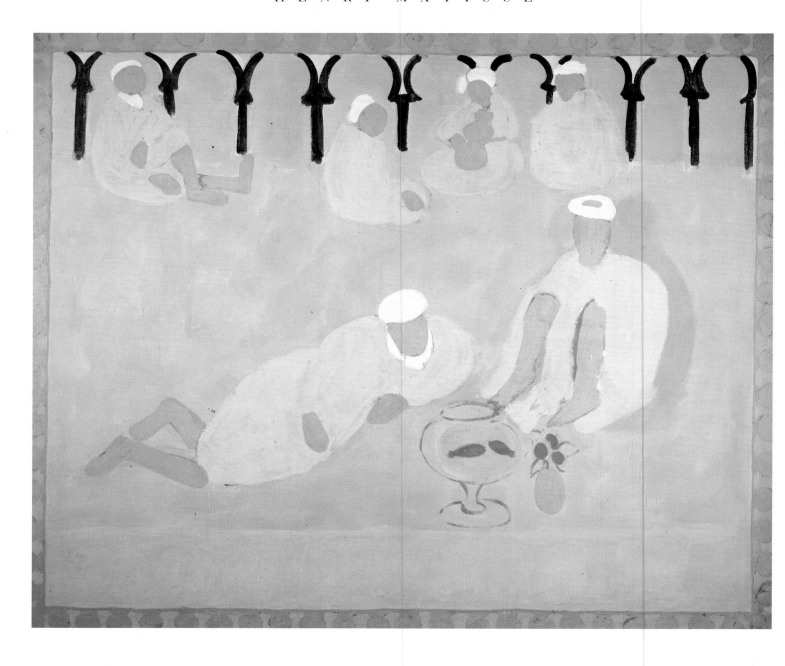

ABOVE
**Arab Café,** 1913
*Distemper on canvas, 69¼×82¾ inches (176×210cm)*
Hermitage Museum, St Petersburg

RIGHT
**Portrait of Madame Matisse,** 1913
*Oil on canvas, 57⅞×38¼ inches (145×97cm)*
Hermitage Museum, St Petersburg

ABOVE

**Open Window, Collioure,** 1914
*Oil on canvas, 45½×35 inches (116×88cm)*
Musée National d'Art Moderne,
Centre Georges Pompidou, Paris

RIGHT

**Mademoiselle Yvonne Landsberg,** 1914
*Oil on canvas, 58×38½ inches (148.5×98.6cm)*
Philadelphia Museum of Art,
Louise and Walter Arensberg Collection

LEFT
**Composition: The Yellow Curtain,** 1915
*Oil on canvas, 57½×38¼ inches (147.3×97.9cm)*
Private Collection

OVERLEAF
**Bathers by a River,** 1909, 1913 and 1916
*Oil on canvas, 101×152.3 inches (259.7×389.9cm)*
Art Institute of Chicago,
Charles H and Mary F S Worcester Collection, 1953.158

ABOVE
**The Window,** 1916
*Oil on canvas, 57½×45½ inches (146×117cm)*
Detroit Institute of Arts, City of Detroit Purchase

RIGHT
**Greta Prozor,** 1916
*Oil on canvas, 57½×37¾ inches (146×96cm)*
Musée National d'Art Moderne,
Centre Georges Pompidou, Paris

**Tree near Trivaux Pond,** 1916-17
*Oil on canvas, 36½×29¼ inches (92.7×74.2cm)*
Tate Gallery, London

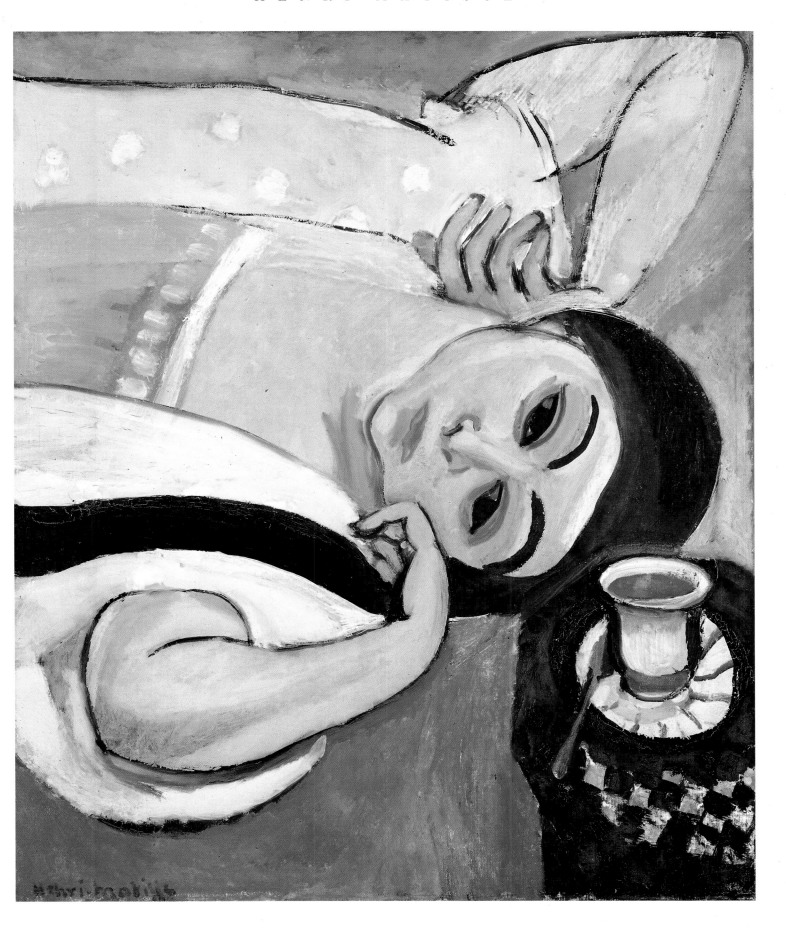

**Head of Laurette and a Cup of Coffee,** 1917
*Oil on canvas, 36¼×28¾ inches (92×73cm)*
Kunstmuseum Solothurn

LEFT

**The Painter and his Model,** 1917
*Oil on canvas, 57⅝×38³/₁₆ inches (146.5×97cm)*
Musée National d'Art Moderne,
Centre Georges Pompidou, Paris

ABOVE
**My Room at the Beau-Rivage,** 1918
*Oil on canvas, 29×23⅞ inches (73.7×60.6cm)*
Philadelphia Museum of Art, A E Gallatin Collection

**Self-Portrait,** 1918
*Oil on canvas, 25⅝×21¼ inches (65×54cm)*
Collection Musée Matisse, Le Cateau-Cambrésis

**Plaster Torso and Bouquet of Flowers,** 1919
*Oil on canvas, 44½×34¼ inches (113×87cm)*
Museu de Arte de São Paolo Assis Chateaubriand

**The Artist and his Model,** 1919
*Oil on canvas, 23⅝×28¾ inches (60×73cm)*
Private Collection

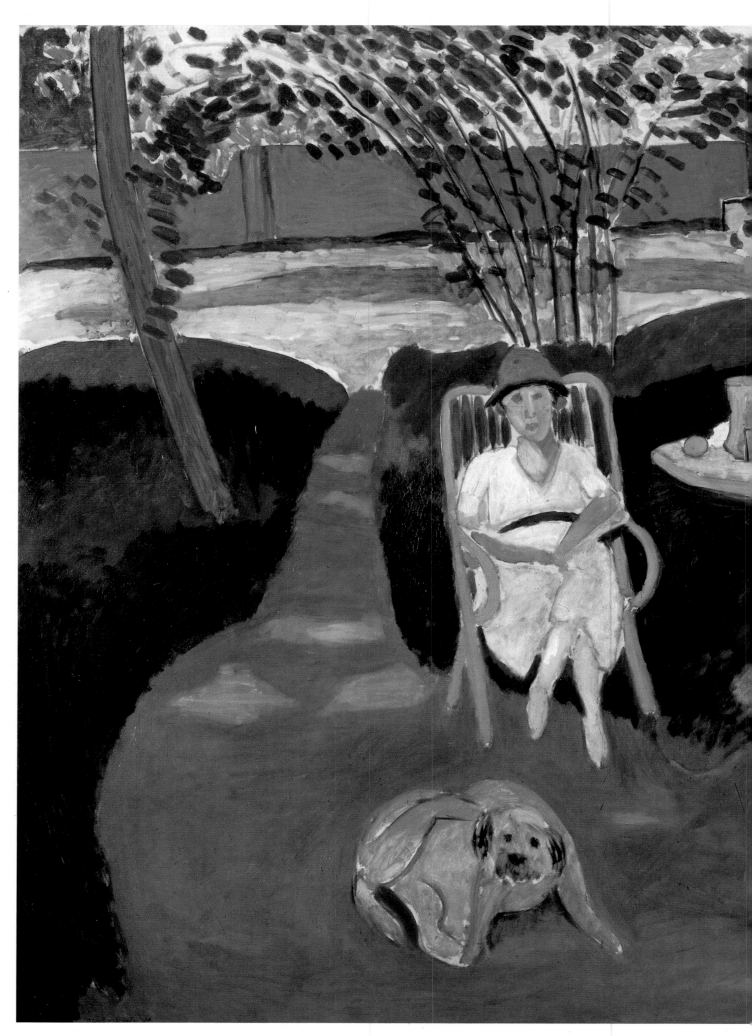

PREVIOUS PAGES
**Tea,** 1919
*Oil on canvas, 55³/₁₆×83³/₁₆ inches (140×212cm)*
Los Angeles County Museum of Art, bequest of David L
Loew in memory of his father Marcus Loew

RIGHT
**Woman before an Aquarium,** 1921-23
*Oil on canvas, 31½×39 inches (80.7×100cm)*
The Art Institute of Chicago,
Helen Birch Bartlett Memorial Collection, 1926.220

ABOVE
**Still Life: Bouquet of Dahlias and White Book,** 1923
*Oil on canvas, 19³/₄×24 inches (50.2×61cm)*
Baltimore Museum of Art, The Cone Collection, formed by
Dr Claribel Cone and Miss Etta Cone of Baltimore, Maryland

RIGHT
**Odalisque, Half-length, The Tattoo,** 1923
*Oil on canvas, 14×9⁵/₈ inches (35.6×24.4cm)*
National Gallery of Art, Washington, Chester Dale Collection

**The Anemones,** 1924
*Oil on canvas, 28¾×36¾ inches (73×92cm)*
Kunstmuseum, Berne

LEFT
**Decorative Figure
on an Ornamental Background,** 1925-26
*Oil on canvas, 51¹/₈×38½ inches (130×98cm)*
Musée National d'Art Moderne,
Centre Georges Pompidou, Paris

ABOVE
**The Yellow Dress** 1929-31
*Oil on canvas, 39³/₈×32 inches (99.7×80.7cm)*
Baltimore Museum of Art, The Cone Collection, formed by
Dr Claribel Cone and Miss Etta Cone of Baltimore, Maryland

**Odalisque,** 1928
*Oil on canvas, 21¼×25⅝ inches (54×65cm)*
Moderna Museet, Stockholm

**Nature Morte au Buffet Vert,** 1928
*Oil on canvas, 32⅛×39⅜ inches (81.5×100cm)*
Musée National d'Art Moderne,
Centre Georges Pompidou, Paris

**Large Reclining Nude,** 1935
*Oil on canvas, 26×36½ inches (66×92.7cm)*
Baltimore Museum of Art, The Cone Collection, formed by
Dr Claribel Cone and Miss Etta Cone of Baltimore, Maryland

**Dance I,** 1931-33

*Oil on canvas,*
*Left panel 133⅞×152¾ inches (340×387cm)*
*Right panel 139¾×196⅛ inches (333×391cm)*
*Center panel 131⅛×154 inches (355×498cm)*

**Detail: center panel**

Musée National d'Art Moderne, Centre Georges Pompidou, Paris

**Nu au Fauteuil, Plante Verte,** 1937-39
*Oil on canvas, 28½×25½ inches (72.5×60.5cm)*
Musée Matisse, Nice

114

**Lady in Blue,** 1937
*Oil on canvas, 36½×29 inches (92.7×73.6cm)*
Philadelphia Museum of Art, Gift of Mrs John Wintersteen

**Music,** 1939
*Oil on canvas, 45¼×45¼ inches (115.2×115.2cm)*
Albright-Knox Gallery, Buffalo, Room of Contemporary Art Fund, 1940

**Interior with Etruscan
Vase,** 1940
*Oil on canvas, 29×39½
inches (73.6×108cm)*
The Cleveland Museum of Art,
Gift of the Hanna Fund,
52.153

**Interior, Yellow and Blue,** 1946
*Oil on canvas, 45¾×32 inches (116×81cm)*
Musée National d'Art Moderne,
Centre Georges Pompidou, Paris

**Polynesia, la Mer,** 1946
*Gouache and cut paper, 77¹/s×123⁵/s inches (196×314cm)*
Musée National d'Art Moderne,
Centre Georges Pompidou, Paris

**The Sorrow of the King,** 1952
*Gouache on paper cut-out,*
*115¼×152 inches (292.7×386cm)*
Musée National d'Art Moderne,
Centre Georges Pompidou, Paris

ABOVE
**Interior with Egyptian Curtain,** 1948
Oil on canvas, 45¾×35⅛ inches (116.2×89.2cm)
The Philips Collection, Washington DC

RIGHT
**Zulma,** 1950
*Gouache and crayon on paper cut-out,*
*93¾×52⅜ inches (238×133cm)*
Statens Museum for Kunst, Copenhagen

HMATISSE 52